1. Probably no single locale is more firmly identified with a group of fighting men than is Iwo Jima with the US Marine Corps. That tiny speck of volcanic ash, five miles long by two and a half at its widest, took a month of bitter fighting and over 22,000 Marine casualties to subdue. The first assault waves found only the barest protection behind terraces of black sand. Behind them Mount Suribachi seemed to smoulder from the effects of three days of naval bombardment. (USMC)

UNIFORMS ILLUSTRATED No 11

US MARINES
in World War Two

ROBERT C. STERN

ARMS AND ARMOUR PRESS

Introduction

Published in 1985 by Arms and Armour Press,
2–6 Hampstead High Street, London NW3 1QQ.

Distributed in the United States by
Sterling Publishing Co. Inc., 2 Park Avenue,
New York, N.Y. 10016.

British Library Cataloguing in Publication Data:
Stern, Robert C.
US marines in World War Two. – (Uniforms
illustrated; no. 11)
1. United States. *Marine Corps* – Uniforms
I. Title   II. Series
359.9′614′0973   VE403
ISBN 0-85368-750-1

Editing, design and artwork by Roger Chesneau.
Typesetting by Typesetters (Birmingham) Ltd.
Printed in Italy by Tipolitografia G. Canale
& C. S.p.A., Turin, in association with Keats
European Ltd.

◀2
2. A BAR (Browning Automatic Rifle) man moves
through the jungle at Cape Gloucester, 8 January
1944. The BAR was a light machine gun that fired the
same .30-06 round as the M1 Garand and
M1917/M1919 machine guns from a 20-round box
magazine at the rate of 500 rounds per minute. Whilst
the availability of such firepower was beneficial, the
BAR was big and complex and too heavy to fire at the
shoulder from a standing position, making it
considerably less effective than later assault rifles.
(USMC)

Most nations' armed forces have small bodies of élite troops whose
traditions and training combine to earn them a reputation for
extraordinary toughness in battle, but only in the rarest conjunctions
of time and place will an entire branch of service gain such repute.
One such instance was the US Marine Corps in the Second World
War.

Beginning in the Revolutionary War as tiny corps of shipborne
riflemen modelled closely after the Royal Marines, the Corps evolved
slowly into a formidable land force that proved its mettle at Belleau
Wood and the Meuse-Argonne. Indeed, its very success in the First
World War threatened its continued existence as a separate entity: the
Army wanted to control all land forces and the Navy saw no place in
its structure for a strictly land-based outfit. Only by redefining the
role of the Marine Corps could it survive as an independent force.
Fortunately, a cadre of Marine officers correctly surmised that the
next war would be fought in the Pacific over tiny islands separated by
vast expanses of ocean. They urged the transformation of the Marine
Corps into a specialized amphibious force, trained and equipped to
seize and hold defended beach-heads. (To understand the boldness of
this view, it is important to remember that this was being proposed in
the 1920s when the conventional wisdom, based on the experience at
Gallipoli, held that an assault on a defended shore was doomed to
failure.) Thus, while diplomats fumbled through a *danse macabre* of
disarmament and appeasement in the 1920s and 1930s, the Marine
Corps quietly sharpened its amphibious skills. At the same time
prototypes of the essential hardware that became
LCMs and LCVPs and Roebling tractors that became LVTs, were
being perfected.

The outbreak of war found the Corps still small, the 1st Marine
Division being still only in the process of formation. By the war's end
six Marine divisions were poised to lead the assault on the Japanese
home islands. Along the way they had suffered 91,000 battle
casualties on jungle islands and coral atolls with strange names. Some,
like Guadalcanal and Iwo Jima, stand in memory as examples of
courage and sacrifice with few equals in history. Some, like Peleliu,
stand in retrospect as wasteful sideshows in the advance across the
Pacific. In all cases, as Admiral Nimitz said about Iwo Jima,
'Uncommon valour was a common virtue'.

A few notes on the weaponry and uniforms to be seen in these pages
are probably in order. Because the campaigns described here were
almost exclusively hot-weather actions, Marine uniforms tended to be
simple and consistent. From Guadalcanal on Marines fought in their
basic dungaree utility tunic and trousers, sometimes camouflaged but
more often green. Each Marine's native resourcefulness often added a
variety of individual touches. Weaponry tended to be what was left
over after the Army got their pick. Bolt-action '03 Springfields, for
instance, are seen in Marine hands long after they had disappeared
from Army service. Because almost all their campaigns were fought
on small islands, Marines are rarely seen carrying full pack gear: in
combat they seldom carried much more than ammunition, a knife and
a canteen or two.

Some of the individuals seen in the accompanying photos are not
Marines at all but Navy personnel seconded to Marine service. For
the most part, 'non-combat' support for Marine activities during the
Second World War, including medical, logistic and heavy engineering
support, was provided by the Navy. All medical personnel, from
corpsmen to field surgeons, were seconded from the Navy. Stories of
heroism under fire of Navy corpsmen are common among the
Marines. All landing craft, with the exception of LVTs, were manned
by naval personnel. Pre-invasion beach clearance was the dangerous
duty of Navy UDTs (Underwater Demolition Teams). Finally, all
heavy engineering was the responsibility of 'Seabees' (CBs, or
Construction Battalions).

Robert C. Stern

3. If there were such a thing as a typical Marine, it might be this man taking a break on Cape Gloucester, 26 December 1943. Even in relaxation his eyes scan the tree-tops for snipers and his right hand has a grip on the sling of his M1 Garand. (USMC)

4. In November 1941 the 4th Marines were pulled out of Shanghai and sent to reinforce MacArthur's meagre garrison in the Philippines. They disembarked at Olongapo, Subic Bay, a scant two battalions – barely 750 officers and men. They are wearing standard prewar khaki cotton utilities except for those assigned stevedore duty who wear blue denim overalls. (USMC)

5. The 1st Battalion, 4th Marines, was immediately posted to Mariveles at the tip of the Bataan Peninsula. Officers of that unit are seen here waiting with their gear at Mariveles for further transport to Corregidor. They all wear pistol belts of khaki webbing from each of which hangs a canteen. The officer on the left has a leather field glass case hanging at his right side, whilst the officer on the far right has a map case on his left hip. (USMC)

◄3

▲6   ▼7

6. As the invading Japanese approached the American positions on Bataan, these 4th Marines traded their peaked service caps for prewar-style steel helmets (virtual copies of the British First World War helmet, distinguished by an embossed Marine 'globe and anchor' emblem at the front). (USMC)

7. Except for two batteries of anti-aircraft guns, the 4th Marines watched the continuing assault on Bataan from the relative safety of Corregidor Island in Manila Bay. When Bataan fell on 9 April 1942, the 105 men of those two batteries were the only Marines among the 75,000 Americans and Filipinos who fell into Japanese hands; they were sent to prisoner-of-war camps in the now infamous 'Bataan Death March'. (USMC)

8. Much of the amphibious doctrine developed by the Marines in the 1930s was modelled broadly on Japanese practice. The 4th Marines got an opportunity to witness a Japanese landing when Corregidor was invaded on 5 May 1942. After twelve hours of bitter fighting, the island surrendered. The 4th suffered over 600 casualties, and 1,283 men were taken prisoner. (USMC)

9. After the disastrous first months of the war, the desire to strike back permeated American planning. One manifestation was the formation of a pair of hand-picked Marine Raider Battalions, the intention being that they would be sent on hit-and-run, commando-style raids against isolated Japanese island outposts. In the event, only one such raid was actually made, against Makin Atoll in the Gilberts on 17–18 August 1942 by Lt. Col. Evans Carlson's 2nd Marine Raider Battalion. This photograph shows Raiders on the submarine *Argonaut* (SS-166) immediately following the conclusion of the raid. They are wearing the new green herring-bone twill dungaree utilities that would be the standard Marine combat uniform for the rest of the war. The loose-fitting tunic is stencilled with the letters 'USMC' and the globe-and-anchor insignia on the single breast pocket. The Raider in the centre wears a pistol belt with clip pouches and an additional cloth bandolier of ammunition pouches around his waist. Note the M1 steel helmets, adopted in 1942. (USN/NARS)

10. Lt. Col. Carlson, seen here on board *Argonaut* after the raid, was one of the more colourful characters produced by the Marines: a veteran of the Nicaraguan Intervention and of China, he was a man whose ideas were too unconventional for most of his superiors. While in China for the third time in 1937, for example, he had travelled on his own initiative to Yenan to observe the Chinese Communists. He came back much impressed with their guerrilla tactics, but, unable to interest the Corps in establishing guerrilla-type units, he resigned to lecture as a private citizen on the need to support China's war against Japan. Convinced that war was inevitable, he rejoined the Marines in April 1941. His first assignment was to travel to England to observe the activities of British Commando units, and his enthusiastic report was the immediate impetus for the creation of the Marine Raiders. Despite his abilities, this raid was Carlson's only official combat command. (USN/NARS)

11. Makin burns as *Argonaut* leaves the scene on 18 August 1942. The raid itself had been less than a total success. The entire enemy garrison had been killed or forced to flee to other islands, but poor communications and inexperience caused a raid that was intended to last one night to stretch out over almost two days, and nine live Raiders, as well as most of the dead, were left behind. Despite this equivocal success, the raid was greeted with wild enthusiasm by a victory-starved public. The long-range results were disastrous because the raid on Makin alerted the Japanese to the weakness of their positions in the Gilbert Islands: when the Marines came back to the Gilberts, they would find vastly strengthened defences. (USN/NARS)

12. One reason for staging the Makin Raid in August 1942 was to distract Japanese attention from the other, much more significant move by Marines in that same month. Alarmed by enemy activity in the Solomons, Allied planners decided to invade Tulagi, where the Japanese had completed a seaplane base, and Guadalcanal, where they were finishing a short airstrip. The 1st Division under Maj. Gen. Alexander Vandegrift was assigned the task of capturing the airstrip on Guadalcanal; Lt. Col. 'Red Mike' Edson's 1st Raider Battalion was to land on Tulagi. Both landings went smoothly on the morning of 7 August 1942; Edson's Raiders, seen here landing on Tulagi, secured the island the next day. (USN/NHC)

13. The battle for Guadalcanal took six months to resolve. Although the airstrip, soon to be named Henderson Field, was captured during the afternoon of the invasion, it would be months before it was truly secure from enemy counter-attack. The fight to push back the enemy was slow and bloody. Here four Marines haul a sniper victim out of the jungle, October 1942. All wear standard dungaree utilities except the man on the right rear of the stretcher who wears a green two-pocket shirt with epaulettes of unknown provenance. (USMC)

▲10   ▼11

12▲   13▼

▲14 ▼15

16 ▲

14. A Marine sits in front of his tent inspecting his bolt-action '03 Springfield, Guadalcanal, 1943. This pre-First World War rifle fired the same .30-06 round as the M1 Garand which did not see widespread use by the Marines until well into 1943. The dungaree trousers came in one length – too long! Most Marines solved the problem by rolling them up. (USMC)

15. Gunners man a 75mm pack howitzer firing towards Japanese positions on Guadalcanal, October 1942. Only one of the Marines in this view is wearing a shirt, which is not surprising considering the heat and humidity of the Solomons. At least two of the Marines sport a globe-and-anchor tattoo, considered by some to be an essential part of the uniform. (USMC)

16. Corpsmen and a chaplain minister to a wounded Marine near the Matanikau River, Guadalcanal, October 1942. Navy corpsmen wore Marine uniforms and were visually indistinguishable from the Marines they served. (USMC)

▲17 ▼18

17. The Matanikau River formed the western front line with the Japanese almost from the beginning of the campaign. The Japanese continued to land fresh troops on their side of the river, and Vandegrift wanted to send raids across the river to disrupt enemy activities, but the first two-battalion raid was a costly failure. A second attempt came in early October when five battalions of Marines under 'Red Mike' Edson and 'Chesty' Puller crossed the Matanikau and swept through the Japanese forces on the far side. (USMC)

18. A pair of Marines guards a ridgeline in Guadalcanal with an M1919 .30 calibre Browning machine gun. They can relax now because Japanese attacks almost always came at night. The Marine in the foreground wears the prewar utility shirt with two flapped breast pockets; on his lap is his personal weapon, a .45 calibre Thompson sub-machine gun. The 'Tommy gun' was used in large numbers by Marines throughout the war, and this one is unusual only in that it has the rarely seen drum magazine. (USMC)

19. After securing Guadalcanal, the Marines next tried to capture the Japanese airfield at Munda on New Georgia Island. This campaign was poorly planned: instead of attacking Munda directly, the 1st Raider Battalion was sent on foot through miles of jungle trails in an attempt to cut off Munda's supply routes at Bairoko prior to the final assault, but the Japanese were not fooled, stubbornly defending every village along the path. In between were scores of swollen jungle streams like this one near Enogai Point, each a potential defensive line for the slowly retreating enemy. July 1943. (USMC)

19▼

▲20

20, 21. The 1st Marine Paratroop Regiment was used for the next step up the Solomons 'ladder' to Rabaul. Instead of assaulting well-defended Kolombangara, the paratroopers were sent against lightly held Vella Lavella on 4 October 1943. They are seen here pushing off from Guadalcanal in LCVPs (Higgins boats) *en route* to Vella, which was taken easily. These paratroopers were the first to receive jungle camouflaged uniforms. Their utilities differed in design from standard only in having extra thigh pockets in the trousers. (USMC)

22. A corpsman gives blood plasma to a wounded Marine while a second looks on, at the base of Tarawa's Long Pier, 22 November

▼21

1943. The utilities worn by the Marine on the left are still almost new, as evidenced by their dark green appearance; as they weathered, the blue in the dye faded, giving them a muddy brown colour. (USMC)

23. An enlisted cameraman in camouflage utilities and fatigue cap films a meeting of I MAC (Marine Amphibious Corps) Engineers officers on Bougainville, December 1943. These engineers wear a mixture of camouflage utilities and Navy khakis. Note the difference in colour between a new camouflage tunic (left) and the more weathered examples. (USMC)

▲24 ▼25

24. Four weary Marines pose amid the debris of battle, Guam, June 1944. In the tropics, the baggy dungaree trousers were rarely bloused into leggings or socks, instead being worn loose or even, like those of the Marine on the right, rolled up to mid-calf. (USMC)

25. A gun crew mans a 37mm anti-tank gun on Guam, July 1944. Like virtually all Marine equipment, the gun has been painted forest green, a colour similar to British bronze green and much darker and bluer than US Army olive drab. The yellow diamond identifies this gun as belonging to the 3rd Marine Division. (USMC)

26. Another assault in LCVPs, this time by the 2nd Raider Regiment supporting the 3rd Division's landing at Cape Torokina, Empress Augusta Bay, Bougainville, on 1 November 1943. Like the paratroopers, the raiders were early recipients of camouflaged utilities, which, except for the patterned cloth, were identical to the green utilities that first appeared at Guadalcanal, even down to the stencilling on the breast pockets. Note also the appearance of the M1 Garand and M1 Carbine, which by now had begun to replace the '03 Springfield as the standard shoulder arm. (USMC)

27. The 3rd Division found two stubborn enemies at Torokina – the Japanese and the mud; there was some debate as to which presented more problems. This Marine light mortar squad slogs through knee-deep mire on its way to the front. The mortarmen carry their personal weapons and some parts of the mortar as well: the Marine fourth from the right, for example, has the 60mm mortar tube slung from his right shoulder. In addition, each man carries at least one bag of mortar rounds. (USMC)

26▲ 27▼

19

▲ 28

▲ 29   ▼ 30

28. A rocket platoon advances at Torokina, November 1943. Each of these Marines carries a single M8A2 4.5in rocket except for the man in the middle who has the rather primitive single trough launcher. Note the camouflaged canvas leggings worn by two members of the platoon. The Bougainville campaign was the first occasion on which rockets were used by the Marines. (USMC)

29. When the Japanese retreated from positions in jungle terrain they often left snipers behind, in order to cause as much havoc as possible; even behind the lines it was always necessary for the US forces to keep an eye on the tree-tops until an area was 'mopped up'. (USMC)

30. 'Mopping up' was often as dangerous as a full-scale battle. This pair of 3rd Division Marines is searching for hidden enemies behind the front line at Torokina, November 1943. The Marine in the foreground with the Garand has a string net helmet cover in place of the more common cloth cover. The junior officer in the background carries a Colt .45 calibre automatic pistol, standard issue to Marine officers since before the First World War, and note also the Bowie knife in the frog hanging from his belt – another traditional piece of Marine equipment. (USMC)

31. A company of 3rd Division Marines prepares to move up the Piva trail soon after landing at Torokina, November 1943. The Marine in the foreground carries multiple 60mm mortar rounds in their protective cardboard tubes. (USMC)

32. The Solomons campaign had as its aim the neutralization of Rabaul, the securing of convoy routes to Australia and the protection of the right flank of MacArthur's drive toward the Philippines. The direct asssault on Japan, however, had to come through the Central Pacific, and the first step on that path was taken when Marines returned to the Gilberts in force with the invasion of Tarawa Atoll on 20 November 1943. Betio Island was approximately 2 square miles of coral defended by 2,600 Japanese troops, 200 guns and a squad of light tanks dug in behind a coconut-log sea wall. The first assault waves of the 2nd Division bravely tried to push inland from the beach in the face of withering defensive fire. (USMC)

▲33

▲34   ▼35

33. Equipped with fewer than 200 Amtracs (LVTs) and supported by insufficient naval gunpower, most of the invaders soon found themselves pinned down behind the sea wall on Red Beach 3. Here a Marine strips belts of .30 calibre ammunition from a dead comrade; the time for sorrow would come later. (USMC)

34. Only in isolated pockets were Marines able to push beyond the sea wall on D-Day; in other areas of the beach-head, movement beyond the wall became impossible. A few brave individuals tried to advance in these areas and others, equally as brave, went out to retrieve the wounded. (USMC)

35. The onshore commander, Lt. Col. David Shoup (the short figure in the middle with the map case) issues orders from his command post on Red Beach 2 on D-Day, 20 November 1943. Reclining at his feet is the ubiquitous Col. Evans Carlson. Present only as an observer from the still-forming 4th Division, Carlson seemed to pop up wherever the action was hottest, rescuing the wounded and leading ashore men pinned down on the reef. Shoup won the Medal of Honor for his leadership on Tarawa, and he went on to become Commandant of the Marine Corps before his retirement in 1963. (USMC)

36, 37. During the first night on Tarawa the Marines consolidated their isolated beach-heads and, beginning at dawn on the 21st, they began the bloody task of reducing the Japanese strongpoints one at a time. Every mound of sand hid a bombproof shelter which would probably contain a few dozen defiant enemy soldiers. The lack of cover made assaults very dangerous, and the defenders rarely surrendered. What appear to be two white bars on the back of the Marine's helmet in photograph 36 is in reality a piece of paper held in place by a rubber band. (USMC)

38. The leaders of the 2nd Division gathered on Tarawa after the last resistance was eliminated on 23 November 1943. On the right is Maj. Gen. Julian Smith, CO of the division. All wear standard Marine utilities, in marked contrast to the often specially tailored uniforms worn by general officers in other branches of service. The only indications of rank are the stars on their collars. (USMC)

39, 40. The last stop for Marines in the drive to isolate Rabaul was Cape Gloucester, New Britain. Marines of the veteran 1st Division hit the 'beach' from LCIs the day after Christmas, 1943. The dense jungle growth hindered the defenders more than the Marines and the initial stages of the landing went smoothly. (USMC)

▲38 ▼39 40▶

▲ 41   ▼ 42

41. After easily capturing Target Hill in front of Yellow Beach on D-Day, Marines line up for chow late on the 26th. As soon as the enemy stopped firing, helmets gave way to the popular fatigue caps. (USMC)

42. The bitterest fighting on Cape Gloucester began with the assault on the two airfields there, which started on 27 December. A few short miles of some of the densest jungle to be found anywhere separated the beach-head from the airfields, and the fight was over possession of individual tree trunks. Here a Marine rifleman peers over a fallen palm log. Additional clips for his M1 Garand hang in a cloth bandolier at his waist. (USMC)

43. The M1 Garand was a clip-fed, semi-automatic .30 calibre rifle that was extremely popular with American troops. Its chief drawbacks were related to its clip-loading system: when a clip was emptied, it was ejected with a loud clang, informing any nearby enemy that a rifleman was at least momentarily out of bullets, and the design of the ten-round clips made it impossible to 'top up' the load with individual rounds. The system's saving grace was that reloading was a fast and simple process. (USMC)

44. The crew of an 81mm mortar, in various states of *déshabillé*, fires at the airfields' defenders at Cape Gloucester, 29 December 1943. The number of ready rounds lying around indicate a prolonged barrage. Two canteens and a helmet lie close at hand in the foreground. (USMC)

43▲   44▼

▲ 45 ▼ 46

45. Fighting in jungle of the density found on Cape Gloucester tested the nerves of even the bravest: seeing, much less identifying, moving shapes only feet away was often impossible (there are *six* Marines 'visible' in this photograph!). Even the machete carried on the pack of the Marine lying in the foreground was of little use here. (USMC)

46, 47. Every jungle stream was contested by invisible enemy riflemen on the far bank. Fortunately, by this time the importance of armour support was well appreciated by the Marines, who in

photograph 46 are waiting for a Sherman tank to appear (note the rear corner of an M4A1 at the far right); after the tank has cleared a path, the riflemen advance. Equally fortunately, the Japanese had no effective anti-tank defence at Cape Gloucester. (USMC)

48. Led by a squad of M4A1 Shermans, Marines stormed the airfields at Cape Gloucester on 31 December 1943, and with their capture the strategic objective was achieved. However, two more weeks of bitter fighting remained before Japanese resistance in the area was effectively eliminated. (USMC)

▲ 49 ▼ 50

49. The last battle in the Cape Gloucester campaign was the capture of Hill 660 by the 7th Marines on 16 January 1944. Here one Marine dozes during a lull in that final assault, seated on his helmet and cradling his M1 Garand; a companion keeps watch, his helmet on his knee and his finger on the trigger of his Thompson. (USMC)

50. After the capture of Hill 660, isolated pockets of resistance remained and a few more Marines lost their lives before the area was completely secure. This raft-load of Marines on the Natamo River was ambushed just minutes after this photograph was taken and two were killed. The Marine at the bow is armed with a BAR; the rest appear to have M1 Garands. February 1944. (USMC)

51. The next target in the Central Pacific campaign was Kwajelein Atoll in the Marshalls. Namur Island was the most stubbornly defended in the atoll, but even there the intensity of the defence never approached that experienced on Tarawa. The 24th Marines of the 4th Division landed on Namur on 1 February 1944. Here a heavy machine-gun team sets up its .50 calibre Browning M2 just up from the beach. The semi-circular insignia on the gun and on the back of the tunic of the loader represents the 4th Division. The gunner still wears his inflatable belt and light pack, not having had a chance to discard them. (USMC)

52. A command team on Namur at a field CP. The Marine on the left has the 4th Division semi-circle stencilled on the back both of his utility tunic and of his trousers. The three numbers within the semi-circle stood for (left to right) the regiment, the battalion and the company of the wearer, '431' indicating that this Marine is a member of the HQ company of the 3rd Battalion of the 24th Marines. The single numeral above the semi-circle indicated the wearer's rank, '4' standing for Lieutenant. The use of this system of identification was very inconsistent: some divisions never adopted it whilst others, like the 4th, used it extensively. Its primary advantage was that it allowed rapid identification of officers in combat. (USMC)

51▲ 52▼

▲ 53

53. A heavy machine-gun squad follows an M3 75mm GMC inland on Namur, 2 February 1944. Note, again, the divisional insignia on both the tunic and the ammunition box of the nearest Marine. The same code number, '402', appears in both insignia. (USMC)

54. A rifle squad crouches in a shell crater on Namur. The Marine in the right foreground is armed with an M1 Carbine fitted with a grenade launcher; the rest carry Garands. On the more sparsely vegetated islands of the Central Pacific the use of camouflaged utilities was quickly discontinued: only the helmet covers and leggings of this squad are of camouflage material. (USMC)

▼ 54

55. Reinforcements move up during the final stage of the battle on Namur, 2 February 1944. The Marine in the centre carries a bazooka, a launcher for 2.36in anti-tank rockets. The Marine on the right is his loader; he carries four canisters each containing a single M6A1 HEAT rocket. (USMC)
56. The Marianas include the largest and most populous of the islands of the Central Pacific and it was here that the Japanese

decided that the Americans had to be repulsed. Each of the larger islands in the chain was well defended with troops, guns, tanks and aircraft and any American move toward the Marianas would be resisted by the full force of the Imperial Navy as well. When Marines of the 2nd and 4th Divisions assaulted Saipan on 15 June 1944 they were met by stiff, well-organized resistance. (USN/NARS)

▲57

▲58 ▼59

57. Much as at Tarawa, most of the first waves of invaders found themselves trapped on the beach by the intensity of defensive fire but, unlike at Tarawa, there was no sea wall behind which to hide, and casualties were enormous, in particular among officers. By sunset, only half the planned beach-head had been secured. Here Marines cling to the beach while an LVT-4 burns at the shoreline. (USMC)

58. Here, a two-man bazooka team has found a gully for protection against defensive fire. The Marine on the left has an M1 Carbine in his right hand and the tube of the bazooka under his left. His loader carries an M1 Garand and six rounds for the bazooka in their protective canister. Saipan, June 1944. (USN/NARS)

59. Unlike the sandy atolls or jungle swamps so far encountered by the Marines, Saipan was relatively civilized. It had built-up towns, cultivated fields of sugar cane and volcanic ridges laced with easily defended interlocking caves. The centre of the island is dominated by Mount Tapotchau. The 8th Marines, 2nd Division, were ordered to take that mountain on 22 June, but the battle occupied three days before the summit was captured. This Marine, carrying scaling rope over his light pack, is seen during the opening phase of that assault. (USN/NARS)

60. Cpl. F. E. Wilbur comes about as close as possible to representing a typical Marine as he leans up against a tree for a smoke during a lull in the fighting on Guam, July 1944. His light pack with rolled-up shelter half, pistol belt and M1 carbine all lie at his side. His camouflage utilities have faded to the point that the pattern can barely be distinguished. (USMC)

61. A pair of 6th Division Marines set up housekeeping at the northern tip of Okinawa, 6 May 1945; the tent is made up of their two new shelter halves (note the strong pattern). The forest green T-shirt was popular clothing during hot weather. (USMC)

▲62 ▼63

62. Marines from 'C' Company, 1st Battalion, 7th Marines, watch over a wounded colleague inside Naha, Okinawa, 11 May 1945. The colour of their faded utilities blends remarkably well into the rubble in the background. (USMC)
63. A mortar squad, part of 'L' Company, 3rd Battalion, 7th Marines, at work on Okinawa, 11 May 1945. The Marine on the right has acquired some high-top 'paratrooper' boots (highly prized items of footwear), into which he has tucked his dungaree trousers. (USMC)
64. Marines near the summit of Mount Tapotchau, 25 June 1944. This view looks south across 'Death Valley' (so named because of the ferocity of the Japanese defence) towards Magicienne Bay. (USN/NARS)

64 ▶

▲ 65

65. A pair of tired Marines take a break and heat some water for coffee on Saipan, June 1944. Each full unit of K-rations contained a small can of 'sterno', a solid alcohol-based fuel designed to burn slowly, sufficient to heat a canteen cup of water to boiling. (USN/NARS)

66. Where there is no wall socket, nor wall for that matter, power to run a field radio is provided by a hand-cranked generator. Saipan, June 1944. (USMC)

67. Another Marine at rest finds local fare to satisfy his hunger. He is seated on a Japanese water cask, and behind him are 'three-packs' of canisters of short 75mm shells for pack howitzers. Note the leather watchband with snap-on cover on his wrist. (USN/NARS)

▼ 66   67 ▶

68. The largest town on Saipan, and the centre of Japanese administration in the Marianas, was Garapan. Its capture took two days of fierce house-to-house fighting by the 2nd Marines, 1–2 July 1944. Here a 37mm anti-tank gun has been set up behind an abandoned Japanese truck in the town. (USMC)

69. A pair of 2nd Marines cautiously advances through the wreckage of a corrugated tin shack, Garapan, 1–2 July 1944. (USMC)

70. A Marine races across open ground towards an anti-tank ditch where three of his companions crouch; the Japanese, obviously, are in possession of the tree-line just beyond. It is rare to see Marines in combat with the rolled shelter half strapped over the light pack. Saipan, July 1944.

71. A 37mm anti-tank gun fires from a sugar cane field towards a farmer's shack in the hilly terrain of northern Saipan, 8 July 1944. On the ridge to the right, a company of Marines advances towards the tree-line. This type of hilly, wooded terrain was ideal for defence, making the advance to Marpi Point at the northern tip of Saipan slow and costly. (USN/NARS)

▲68　▼69

72. One of the last points of organized resistance was this cutting for Saipan's narrow-gauge railway through the base of Mount Marpi. Here Marines cautiously probe the cutting, wary of Japanese snipers hidden in the tall grass up the hill, 9 July 1944. On this day the island was declared secure, although pockets of Japanese resistance would be encountered for weeks to come. (USN/NARS)

73. The 'top brass' of the Saipan operation meet at 2nd Division HQ, July 1944. On the left is Lt. Gen. Holland M. ('Howling Mad') Smith, CO of V Amphibious Corps and effective commander of all troops ashore. In the middle is Maj. Gen. T. E. Watson, CO of the 2nd Division, whilst on the right is Admiral Raymond Spruance, CO of the Fifth Fleet and commander of all land and sea forces in the Marianas operation. (USN/NARS)

74. The 3rd Division went ashore on Guam against heavy opposition on 21 July 1944. Originally scheduled for 18 June, the invasion was repeatedly postponed by enemy naval activity and the unexpectedly strong resistance on Saipan. Here Marines crouch on the beach before pushing inland behind an LVT-2. (USMC)

◀72

73▲   74▼

▲ 75

75. Led by an M4A3 Sherman, Marines advance across a grassy field studded with palm trees, Guam, July 1944. Note the signalman (fourth from the left) laying telephone wire as he moves forward with the riflemen. (USMC)

76. Guam, like Saipan, is hilly, with plenty of caves in the limestone ridges in which defenders could hole up. In these first encounters with dug-in Japanese soldiers the Marines began to evolve the tactics they would need on many later islands. While riflemen covered the entrance, another Marine would edge close enough to hurl grenades deep into the cave. Note the cloth bandolier of grenades, generally used for carrying clips for the Garand, over the shoulder of the nearest man. (USMC)

▼ 76

77▲

77. Those unlucky enough to be wounded were brought to an aid station manned by Navy corpsmen whose skill saved many a Marine's life. In this photograph, wounded on stretchers wait their turn in the 'surgery', a hastily built structure of ropes, sticks and a camouflaged shelter half, Guam, July 1944. Navy corpsmen dressed identically to the Marines they tended. (USN/NARS)

78. Advancing across a rice paddy, Marines hurl grenades at the Japanese defenders of a tree-line. In general, resistance on Guam was less fierce than on Saipan, but the conquest still took more than two weeks. The island was not declared secure until 10 August 1944. (USN/NARS)

78▼

▲ 79

79. In response to the Japanese habit of leaving snipers behind in areas evacuated by organized forces, the Marines introduced a new defensive weapon: a platoon of Dobermann pinschers and their handlers were employed on Guam for night perimeter security and for hunting snipers. Four dogs and two handlers were killed in the course of the campaign. (USN/NARS)

▼ 80

80. Communications between units ashore were often tenuous at best. Right behind the riflemen came signal company troops laying field telephone lines and behind them came the portable field exchange responsible for getting messages through to their destination. Guam, August 1944. (USN/NARS)

81. Tinian lay across a narrow channel from Saipan, from which it was invaded on 24 July by Marines of the 4th Division. Unlike the landings on Saipan and Guam, the invasion beaches chosen for Tinian were not the obvious ones and the landings therefore took place against only light opposition. This was largely due to the loud advocacy of Col. Evans Carlson who, himself wounded while attempting to rescue wounded Marines on Guam, was now restricted to planning activities on 4th Division staff. (USMC)

82. Marines rest in shell craters while three M4A3 Shermans and an M5A1 Stuart advance across a cabbage field on Tinian. (USMC)

▲ 83 ▼ 84

83. Gunners fire a 75mm pack howitzer directly into caves occupied by Japanese defenders o Tinian. It was assembled on the point of rock from which it fires, having been hauled into place a piece at a time, and is held in position by ropes around the limber. (USMC)

84. Sheltering from a tropical cloudburst on Tinian, Marines exhibit some of the varieties of ra gear available. The two men on th right wear full-length rubberized canvas hooded raincoats; the Marine third from the left wears a short hooded anorak; and the Marine next to him has his standard-issue poncho draped ov his arm. (USN/NARS)

85. Amtracs burn on the reef as Marines crouch behind a DUKW at water's edge on Peleliu, 15 September 1944. Throughout the war in the Pacific, controversy raged over the question of which islands to invade and which to bypass. Probably none was more controversial than the decision to capture Peleliu in the Palaus in support of MacArthur's drive toward the Philippines. The choi of targets up to this point had bee straightforward. However, with t capture of the Marianas, the Allie had broken Japan's outer defensi perimeter and won bases from which to begin the long-range strategic bombing of Japan, and whether or not MacArthur's driv on the Philippines had any bene-ficial effect on the war effort is an unresolved question. What is undeniable is that the capture of Peleliu in no way aided that or an other campaign and cost the 1st Marine Division over 9,000 casualties. (USMC)

86. Marines push up the first ridg line on D-Day, not yet suspectin the ferocity of the cave-by-cave struggle that awaited them. Pelel is a small island, much smaller th any of the Marianas, only two mi by six, and it is entirely dominate by a central spine known as the Umurbrogol, a series of limeston outcrops that was soon dubbed 'Suicide Ridge' by those unfor-tunate enough to fight there. On Peleliu the Japanese tried out a n tactic: contesting the landing onl with artillery, all 10,000 defende remained in their interconnected caves, waiting for the Marines to come to them. There would be n more wasteful 'Banzai' charges, a counter-attacks would be local ar limited. (USMC)

▲ 87   ▼ 88

87. A Marine F4U Corsair drops napalm on a Japanese position on Suicide Ridge. Unfortunately, in this kind of fighting, even the best close air support is of little use. (USMC)

88. Black Marines of the 16th Field Depot push forward on Peleliu, September 1944. While blacks were officially used only as support troops, there often was no clearly defined front line on Peleliu and Marines of the 16th Field Depot often found themselves in combat, winning high praise. (USN/NARS)

89, 90. The battle for Suicide Ridge was a bitter hand-to-hand contest. These two photographs depict one small incident among thousands of similar events. In the first view, one Marine tosses a 'Molotov cocktail' while others watch to see the result; a second has been lit and awaits use in the foreground. Lacking a flamethrower, these petrol bombs were the most effective weapons available against defenders in caves. Two of the Marines are wearing the dark green, standard-weather wear with the dungaree tunic. In the second photograph a wounded man, probably the Marine standing at the top in the first photograph, is eased down. Note the rifle grenade on the Garand in the foreground. (USMC)

▲ 91   ▼ 92

91. A wary Marine peers into a cave mouth still smoking from the explosion of grenades. So many of the caves on Peleliu interconnected that enemy soldiers forced back into one could re-emerge from another. (USN/NARS)

92. A communications team on Peleliu relays messages from radio to field telephone. The Marine in the foreground has a codebook for quick translation of coded radio messages into plain language for telephone communication. (USN/NARS)

93. The battle for Suicide Ridge lasted until 27 November, although the Marines were relieved by Army troops on 15 October, one month after D-Day, and played no further part in the battle. Col. 'Chesty' Puller's 1st Marines suffered 56 per cent casualties in the first week. The standard Marine tactic of pushing forward as fast as possible came under criticism as being inappropriate to this new kind of battle with a cornered enemy unable to retreat and unwilling to surrender. (USN/NARS)

94. As bloody as the conquest of Peleliu had been, it proved to be just a bitter foretaste of the most vicious island campaign and the costliest battle in Marine Corps history – the invasion of Iwo Jima. The island was defended by 23,000 Japanese troops and their defeat would, for the only time, cost the Marines more casualties than were suffered by the enemy. Three Marine Divisions, the 3rd, 4th and new 5th, went ashore on 19 February 1945 on an island even smaller than Peleliu. Its conquest would take 36 days. (USMC)

93▲   94▼

▲ 95   ▼ 96

54

95. Two problems immediately faced the invaders – the coarse black sand of the almost featureless beach and the looming bulk of Mount Suribachi. The former made traction almost impossible for men and machines; the latter dominated the left flank of the beach-head until its conquest on D-Day+4. (USMC)

96. A hasty command conference on Iwo Jima, 20 February 1945. The two officers on the left have M1 Carbines with web clip pouches wrapped around the buttstock, a common field fit. The officer on the right carries his entrenching tool from his belt, a very unusual position. (USMC)

97. An observation post at the foot of Mount Suribachi, Iwo Jima, 22 February 1945. The Marine on the far left is talking into a 'walkie-talkie', a portable personal field radio. Weather colder than any hitherto encountered in the Pacific has caused these Marines to wear multiple layers of clothing. (USMC)

97▼

▲ 98

98. Mount Suribachi fell to the 28th Marines on 23 February. The first flag-raising was a relatively unspectacular affair, employing a small flag carried up by the lieutenant in command of the company that took the summit. The battalion commander wanted to save the historic flag, so he ordered a second, large flag to be raised in the place of the first. This second flag-raising, photographed by AP photographer Joe Rosenthal, has become the image most associated with the Marines. (USMC)

99. The capture of Mount Suribachi represented the beginning rather than the end of the battle of Iwo Jima. These Marines of the 4th Division fight out of a shell crater on the flat Motoyama Plateau in the centre of the island. The Marine on the right, about to heave a grenade, wears an Army M1941 field jacket – a short khaki 'windbreaker' jacket with a pair of slash pockets and epaulettes and a fairly common piece of clothing on Iwo Jima. (USMC)

100. The pile of discarded ammunition boxes and spent shell cases attest to the intensity of the fight for the crew of this water-cooled M1917A1 .30 calibre machine gun. The loader on the right, preparing another box of ammunition, wears a reversed fatigue cap beneath his helmet. (USMC)

101. A column of Sherman tanks advances across the plateau toward the airfields, watched by 4th Division Marines. The man in the fore-ground has the divisional semi-circular insignia stencilled on the back of his tunic. (USMC)

102. Finding shelter from enemy fire in a foxhole on the edge of one of the Motoyama airstrips, this Marine officer is seen using a field telephone. He is wearing an M1941 field jacket. (USMC)

103. A spotting team calls out corrections to a gun crew, Iwo Jima, February 1945. The Marine nearest the camera carries a full load of gear including light pack and folding entrenching tool. Note the Bowie knife in its belt frog. (USMC)

101▶

▼ 102

▲104

105▶

104. A 4th Division field telephone repair crew checks the lines at a junction strip. The Marine in the background has the 4th Division semi-circle stencilled on his helmet cover. (USMC)

105. A comrade helps a Marine who has suffered a head wound, Iwo Jima, February 1945. The injured man wears an M1941 field jacket over his standard dunagree tunic. (USMC)

106. Marine war correspondents enjoy the rare luxury of brushing their teeth, Iwo Jima, February 1945. The Marine in the centre wears a khaki utility shirt with two flapped breast pockets; the others wear standard Marine utilities. Note the .45 calibre pistol in the shoulder holster. (USMC)

107. A Navy corpsman gives blood plasma to a wounded Marine while a 4th Division officer looks on, Iwo Jima, February 1945. The corpsman wears an M1941 field jacket, and the officer wears standard utilities with a hooded anorak under his tunic. The '5' stencilled over the semi-circle indicates the rank of Captain. (USMC)

108. A Jewish chaplain holds Sabbath services on Iwo Jima, February 1945. The variety of uniforms worn by his congregation represents a cross-section of those seen in combat. Only two of the congregants (fourth from the left and second from the right) and the chaplain himself wear standard utilities. Those two congregants have the rectangle representing the 5th Division stencilled on their tunic. The Marines third and fourth from the right wear paratrooper trousers with additional thigh pockets, whilst those on the far left and third from the left wear the Army M1944 jungle tunic with two flapped breast pockets. The Marine second from the left wears a hooded anorak and the man fifth from the left wears a white sweatshirt. The Marine third from the right wears an Army M1942 flannel shirt. (USMC)

109. Okinawa was the last island in Pacific to be invaded by the Marines during the Second World War, and it was by far the largest. The Japanese had learned their lessons well and made no attempt to contest the landings by four American Divisions, two Army and two Marine (the 1st and the new 6th), on 1 April 1945. The 6th Division cleared the northern half of the 60-mile-long island without undue difficulty while the 1st Division and the two Army divisions probed south until they encountered the enemy's defensive line just north of Naha, the island's capital. This photograph shows Marines of the 1st Division relaxing with Ernie Pyle (bare headed, fourth from the left), probably the best known American war correspondent, Okinawa, 8 April 1945. (USMC)

▲ 106   ▼ 107

▲110

▼111

110. The attack on the Shuri Line began on 19 April. It would take a month and ten days before Shuri Castle would fall. These 6th Division Marines are fighting in front of Sugar Loaf Hill, a key feature in the Shuri Line, May 1945. The wooded, mountainous terrain obviously favoured the defences. (USMC)

111. Marines push forward towards Naha. The lead man and the one on the far right wear Army flannel shirts and the former carries a field telephone over his left shoulder and a general-purpose bag over his right. The second Marine (partly hidden) carries a box of K-ration halves. Each man carries his shelter half neatly rolled on his light pack. (USMC)

112. The cave fighting on Peleliu and Iwo Jima led to the evolution of weapons and tactics suited to fighting an enemy entrenched deep in the earth. The primary new weapon was the portable flame-thrower, which fired a burning stream of jellied petrol – devastatingly effective in the confined space of a cave. (USMC)

113. A pair of 6th Division Marines bail out their foxhole which has filled with water despite being covered by two shelter halves. The Marine on the right wears an Army M1941 field jacket over his tunic, Okinawa, May 1945. (USMC)

▲114

114. A wounded Navy corpsman, wearing an Army M1941 field jacket over his utilities, leads a wounded Marine to the rear, Okinawa, May 1945. Corpsmen served in the front lines with the Marines and suffered casualties at a similar rate. (USMC)

115. Once the Shuri Line was broken, the next task was the capture of Naha, which fell to Marines of the 6th Division after bitter fighting in late May 1945. Naha was by far the largest and most built-up city in which Marines had to fight during the Second World War. Here one very cautious Marine peers around the corner of a building while two colleagues look on from safer positions. He has a single M6A3 bazooka round in its protective canister strapped

to his light pack; the Marine in the centre has two bare M6A3 rockets strapped to his pack. (USMC)

116. The co-operation of armour is even more essential than usual in built-up areas, and these 6th Division Marines are content to let the M4A3 Sherman clear a path between buildings in Naha, Okinawa, late May 1945. The square insignia indicates that the tank was attached to the 2nd Division, which was committed on Okinawa only late in the campaign. Armoured units were freely 'swapped' between divisions, being sent where they were needed regardless of unit boundaries. (USMC)

115▲ 116▼

▲117

117. Even after Naha fell to the 6th Division, snipers remained in the rubble and had to be flushed out. Here a squad of Marines supported by an M1919 .30 calibre machine gun prepares to charge a sniper holed up in the wreckage of a temple in Naha, late May 1945. (USMC)

118. Exhausted 6th Division Marines rest in a lane in the suburbs of Naha, late May 1945. The fighting on Okinawa continued in the mountainous peninsulas south of Naha for another month, and the last organized resistance was crushed only on 21 June 1945. Fortunately for these men, and for all the Marines, the invasion of Japan planned to begin in November 1945, which would have involved all six Marine Divisions in its two stages, proved unnecessary. (USMC)

▼ 118